An Introduction to
WILLIAMSBURG

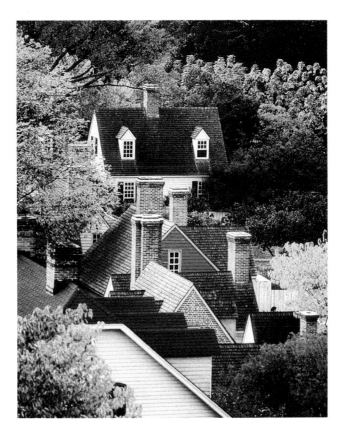

Written by Valerie Tripp

Published in cooperation with
The Colonial Williamsburg Foundation by

Copyright © 1985 by Pleasant Company

ISBN 0-932407-00-5

First Edition.
Printed in the United States of America.
94 95 96 97 98 99 WCR 10 9 8 7 6 5

W alk down Williamsburg's deep-shaded streets and walk back into history. Back to the eighteenth century, when ladies in elegant gowns and gentlemen in powdered wigs rode in horse-drawn carriages down the dusty streets. Back to colonial times, when the king of England ruled America and the British flag flew above the housetops you pass. Back more than two hundred years in the footsteps of George Washington, Thomas Jefferson, and Patrick Henry, to the Williamsburg they knew—a bustling, prosperous place, the lively capital of Virginia, the largest British colony in America.

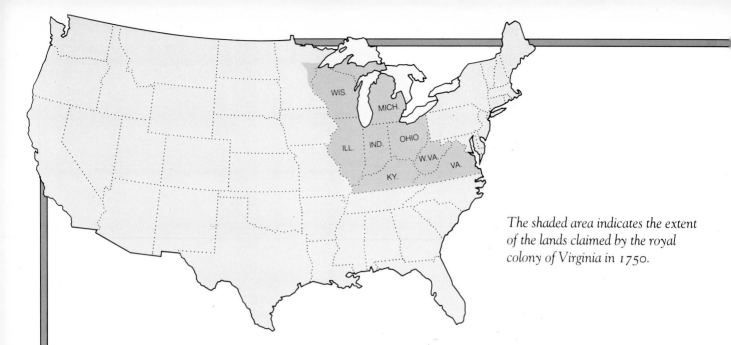

The shaded area indicates the extent of the lands claimed by the royal colony of Virginia in 1750.

Remember as you walk that Williamsburg in its prime was a compact, civilized city on the edge of a vast, untamed continent. The colony of Virginia was much larger than the state of Virginia we know today. It stretched from the Atlantic Ocean west to the Mississippi River and north to the Great Lakes. Like all of the thirteen colonies, Virginia was ruled by the king of England. Colonial Virginians were his subjects, obeying the laws of Parliament and paying taxes to the crown. In fact, from Parliament's point of view, America existed primarily for the economic benefit of the British, who saw the colonies as a growing market for British-made goods and as a rich source of raw materials that could be shipped back to England.

Williamsburg was born as the eighteenth century dawned. The original capital of Virginia had been located in the crowded village of Jamestown. When the statehouse there burned in 1699, the legislators voted to rebuild it in a new place. They named the new town Williamsburg in honor of their king, William III. Here was a chance for a fresh start, the opportunity to create a noble capital city where before there had been little more than fields and forests. To guard against haphazard growth, a town plan was drawn up that was both practical and artistic. Williamsburg's main street was to be long and broad, skirted by wide greens and open spaces. Houses were to be set back six feet from the streets on lots of one-half acre. The main street, named for the Duke of Gloucester, would stretch nearly a mile from the College of William and Mary, past the church and the market square, to the new statehouse called the Capitol. Soon there would be an elegant Palace for the governor of the colony, who was the king's appointed representative there.

By 1750 Williamsburg had become the most important city in Virginia. People came here from remote parts of the colony to learn of the latest fashions from England and Europe in clothing, furnishings, music, amusements, and ideas. It was a major business center where tobacco planters, farmers, craftsmen, shippers, and merchants came to buy, sell, and trade. And because Williamsburg was the capital of Virginia, it was the political center of the colony where affairs of government were conducted. Laws made in the Capitol and enforced in the courts here affected everyone in Virginia and even influenced other colonies far beyond its borders.

As this label indicates, "fine, mild, old" tobacco grown in the rich Virginia soil was a highly valued colonial crop sold in London.

Patrick Henry by Thomas Sully

George Washington by Charles Willson Peale

Thomas Jefferson by Gilbert Stuart

As the century progressed and the colonists prospered, a strong sense of independence began to stir within them. Though their heritage and traditions were deeply rooted in England and their emotional loyalty was to the king, resentment of British rule began to grow. Why should they pay heavy taxes to support a king and country three thousand miles away? Heard first as mild grumblings in shops and taverns, the sentiment gained strength until it rumbled in heated debate within the walls of the Capitol. Finding voice in the impassioned eloquence of Thomas Jefferson, Patrick Henry, and other patriots, the colonists' frustrations finally erupted into the War for Independence.

For a few more years Williamsburg remained the vibrant city it had become. From 1776 to 1780 it was the wartime capital of the new commonwealth of Virginia. But in 1780 the capital was moved once more, this time to Richmond fifty miles away, where it remains to this day. With it went the hustle and bustle, the energy and excitement on which Williamsburg had thrived. With it also went the pressures and problems of economic progress and urban growth. Williamsburg was left behind, allowed to fade slowly into the gentle tranquility of a small college town and county seat.

So it slept until 1926 when Dr. W. A. R. Goodwin, the rector of Bruton Parish Church, inspired John D. Rockefeller, Jr., an industrialist and philanthropist, to restore the colonial capital city to its former glory. Mr. Rockefeller gave the restoration project his personal leadership and funded it generously for the next thirty-four years. Today Williamsburg is a living museum where millions come to learn about life in colonial times and to witness the place where the spirit of American independence took root and grew.

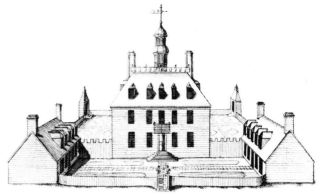

This detail from an engraved copper plate found in the Bodleian Library at Oxford University in England helped architects design the reconstruction of the Governor's Palace.

PEOPLE

Imagine that you are strolling through Williamsburg more than two hundred years ago. Many of the people you see are visitors like yourself, drawn to this place because it is a social, cultural, and commercial center equalled by few other cities in the colony.

As you pass by Market Square, you can't miss the open-air stands set up by farmers from the outskirts of Williamsburg. They hag- gle with servants from fine Williamsburg homes over the prices of cabbages, chickens, and live- stock. A noisy crowd has gathered around a juggler. The laughter distracts the apothecary's appren- tice, who has been sent to the market to buy medicinal herbs. A group of sailors lounging under a tree chat with a frontiersman from western Virginia. Two American Indians watch straight-backed soldiers march by. The soldiers are followed by a rollicking bunch of barefoot little boys.

Stop at John Greenhow's store and you will find quieter, more dignified shoppers. A wealthy to- bacco planter has come to town to sell his crop. He and his wife are in Greenhow's store buying imported delicacies: chocolate, coffee, and tea. The planter's slaves load bags of rice and flour onto a cart. Nearby a merchant's agent waits to deliver a shipment of seeds, spices, and flower bulbs that has just arrived from London.

Back at the King's Arms Tav- ern, the keeper hands you a mug of ale and a plate of oysters. You sit back to read the *Virginia Ga- zette*, a newspaper printed and sold just across the street, but it is hard to concentrate because two burgesses at a nearby table are en-

gaged in such heated debate. They've come from two distant counties in Virginia to attend the General Assembly, which meets here in the Capitol. In the corner two earnest students from the College of William and Mary eavesdrop on their discussion.

Of all the crowd you have seen, remember that most are not permanent residents. In fact, in 1775 only 1,880 people lived year-round in Williamsburg. A disproportionate number of them were upper-class gentry. Because this city was the capital of the king's largest colony, royal appointees, wealthy merchants, and businessmen settled here to conduct business and become involved in local and colonial government. However, the energy and vitality of Williamsburg came not only from those privileged classes but also from the working people who built Williamsburg and made it function. Such citizens as shopkeepers, tavern keepers, and craftspeople made their living by serving the many visitors who came here, as well as the permanent residents. Slightly more than half the residents of Williamsburg were black. While a few of them were free blacks, most were the slaves and servants of the community.

CLOTHING

Eighteenth-century gentry in colonial Williamsburg dressed just as stylishly as their counterparts in London and Paris. At a ball at the Governor's Palace, for example, you would have seen dancers swirl by in elegant clothing made of the best imported fabrics—silk from China, satin and velvet from Europe, fine linen from Ireland—all in bright colors with elaborate patterns, trimmed with embroidery, lace, and artificial flowers. The clothes were beautiful, luxurious, and impractical. They also gave a quick clue to a person's rank in society, for only the privileged who never dirtied their hands would wear ruffled cuffs trimmed with lace.

It was fashionable for women to have small waists, so ladies wore corsets called *stays*, often laced so tightly that the ladies could hardly breathe. To make their waists seem even smaller they wore wooden hoops on their hips to make their skirts stand out. Dresses were cut low in the front and narrow in the shoulders. Fancy dresses worn for special occasions were made of heavily trimmed fabrics and could weigh as much as fifteen pounds, permitting ladies little freedom of movement.

Atop his ruffled shirt a gentleman often wore a tight-fitting waistcoat so that he, too, could have a

Mrs. Thomas Newton, Jr., with child

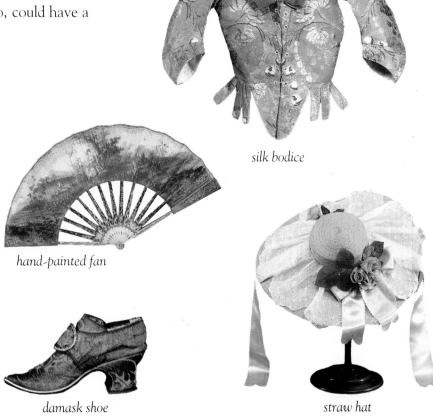

silk bodice

hand-painted fan

damask shoe

straw hat

Mr. Thomas Newton, Jr.

fine figure. Men were proud of their legs and wore breeches that stopped at the knee. Silk stockings and high-heeled shoes showed off their well-turned calves. Coats that came only to the knee had large sleeve cuffs trimmed with braid and buttons.

Babies wore loose dresses until they were about five years old. Young girls dressed like their mothers in stays, hoops, petticoats, and caps. Wealthy boys might dress like their fathers in satin breeches, lacy shirts, and silk brocade coats for fancy occasions.

People who worked every day wore sturdy clothes made of less expensive imported fabrics or homespun, simpler in style and much more practical. Few of these garments have survived, probably because they were worn out. Working women and girls wore simple cotton shifts covered by skirts called *petticoats* and jackets or shortened gowns. In cool weather they may have worn short capes called *tippets*, which came just to the fingertips.

Men and boys wore durable breeches, warm knitted stockings, and stout shoes. A workingman's plain, loose-fitting shirt was sometimes worn open at the neck with the sleeves rolled up above the elbow. For warmth a man might wear a cloak or a great coat and a tricorn, or "cocked" hat.

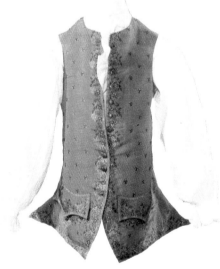

silk waistcoat

man's pocketbook

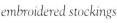

negligee cap

embroidered stockings

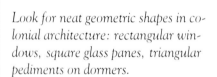

BUILDINGS

Elegant or simple, imposing or cozy, of strong, ruddy brick or clean, white weatherboard, the buildings of Williamsburg form your first and most lasting impression of the place. Look closely at them and you will see tangible evidence of the values of the people who built a new country: a respect for symmetry and beauty, practicality and permanence, individuality and harmony.

Even simple structures called *outbuildings* or *dependencies* reflect these values. Look at the dairy behind Wetherburn's Tavern. It is small, square, and perfectly proportioned. The wavy grillwork under the eaves is a pleasing architectural detail but also provides ventilation to keep the inside cool. The shingles of the roof overlap as delicately as flower petals, giving a charming scalloped effect, but their round butts serve a practical purpose: to keep them from warping.

Stop in front of the George Wythe House or the Brush-Everard House and see how these values were reflected in larger structures built during the eighteenth century. Notice the symmetry in their designs: the same number of windows appears on either side of the door and the upstairs windows are placed directly above those on the first floor.

Because there were no trained architects in eighteenth-century Virginia, most buildings were designed by a gentleman amateur or a master carpenter who followed working instructions published in builders' handbooks. They carried forward the classical architectural tradition of England, adapting it to the new climate and materials available to them. The master carpenter knew the various building requirements that had been specified in the original city charter to insure that each building in Williamsburg contributed to a sense of permanence and order.

Many of the elegant homes and public buildings of Williamsburg have stood for over two hundred years, a reflection of the skill of the craftsmen who built them and the wealth of the owners who could afford the best materials available. Dwellings for slaves and working-class people were often not as carefully built as houses for the well-to-do.

Look for neat geometric shapes in colonial architecture: rectangular windows, square glass panes, triangular pediments on dormers.

They were sometimes constructed without foundation or "earth sunk." Most of these humbler houses were lost over time to fire, decay, and demolition.

Eighty-eight of the original buildings were standing when the restoration of Williamsburg began. Archaeological excavations and historical records helped unearth clues to the structure and function of the others, allowing for the authentic re-creation you see today.

Even the smallest details reflect the colonists' love of geometry and balance. Look under the eaves of colonial homes for a decorative strip of small wood blocks called dentils lined up like a row of teeth.

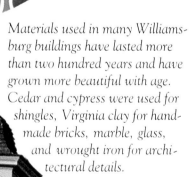

Materials used in many Williamsburg buildings have lasted more than two hundred years and have grown more beautiful with age. Cedar and cypress were used for shingles, Virginia clay for handmade bricks, marble, glass, and wrought iron for architectural details.

FURNISHINGS

You are invited to enter each building of Williamsburg as a welcome guest. The sun streams through the windows. A fire burns on the hearth. A book lies open next to a comfortable chair. It is as if your host has just stepped out for a moment, leaving you to make yourself at home.

Some of the homes you will visit are grand, like those of George Wythe or Peyton Randolph. There, candles in shining brass candlesticks cast a warm glow on polished walnut and mahogany tables and reflect brightly in gilt-framed looking glasses. Because it was fashionable to have furnishings from all over the world, you will see Turkish carpets and Italian silk damask curtains. Room decorations changed with the season in many of the fine homes. In the summer grass floor mats, light seersucker window hangings, and cotton chair covers were used to make the rooms appear cooler. In more modest homes, such as the Geddy House, simpler fabrics were used instead of velvet and silk. Household articles of pottery, brass, copper, and pewter took the place of silver and china.

In fancy and plain rooms some furnishings are surprisingly familiar, like Venetian blinds in Wetherburn's Tavern and an enormous billiard table in the Raleigh Tavern. Some furnishings are unfamiliar. Tables were covered with green felt because writers using quill pens needed a soft surface beneath their paper. A copper bedwarmer filled with hot coals was pushed between the covers to warm the cold sheets. Some furnishings are ingenious. There is a bed that folds against the wall in the office of the Raleigh Tavern keeper, and indoor shutters fold back and disappear into the window casements in the Wythe House.

Such efficient use of space is characteristic of Williamsburg houses. Even in fine homes a room served more than one purpose because it was wasteful to heat and light several rooms unnecessarily. A bedchamber served as a man's office, sleeping space, and dressing room. A lady's bedchamber was her retreat during the day, where she might paint, read, do needlework, or have tea with a friend. The dining room often doubled as a parlor after dinner. A drop-

Williamsburg had a reputation for the excellent cabinet work of its artisans. Furnishings such as this desk-bookcase were found in fine homes alongside imported objects.

Beds were often enclosed with curtains because rooms heated with fireplaces were drafty.

leaf table could be folded into a narrow rectangle and pushed to the side of the room. Dining chairs were moved against the wall so that small tables for cards or chess could be moved in front of the fire for an after-dinner game.

English china teapot

brass spice caster

mahogany dressing box

Brightly colored floor cloths were fashionable in colonial homes, as seen here in the Brush-Everard dining room and in the study of the Peyton Randolph house.

CARDENS & GREENS

Williamsburg's gardens are quiet surprises. They're hidden behind houses. They're glimpsed through picket fences. They're waiting for you to discover them. Walk under an arch cut out of a dense green hedge and the busy street disappears behind you. It's so peaceful in these tucked-away gardens that you feel you've found a secret retreat.

Sit on a bench in the shade of a towering elm tree. You'll feel calmed and refreshed by the neatly clipped grass, carefully pruned boxwood hedges, and orderly beds of flowers. Breathe deeply. Smell the heady aroma of roses and the spicy fragrance of herbs planted in intricate formations. Even hard-working kitchen gardens like the one behind the King's Arms Tavern are pleasant to look at. Beans, squash, corn, peas, and potatoes grow in tidy rows. In gardens throughout the town, fruit trees are full of light blossoms or heavy with plums, peaches, apples, figs, and cherries. Imagine how the same sights must have comforted eighteenth-century citizens who knew Williamsburg was a tiny spot of cultivated order amid a rolling, ragged countryside.

Williamsburg's gardens flourish now as they did in the eighteenth century, when landscaping was a fashionable pursuit in England and the colonies. King William himself enjoyed

Through much of the year Williamsburg's gardens bloom abundantly with tulips, lilies, peonies, periwinkles, hollyhocks, crocuses, and hundreds of other flowers.

designing formal gardens with long elegant vistas—like those behind the Governor's Palace—with arbors, fish ponds, and topiary bushes trimmed into geometrical or animal shapes. Queen Mary, his wife, loved flowers and made them so popular that floral patterns blossomed inside houses on fabrics, china, and wallpaper.

Gardens were private retreats, but public greens like Market Square were lively centers for such community activities as fairs, militia musters, and farmers' markets. It is even possible to think of the entire city of Williamsburg as one enormous park. When the original street plan was laid out, long, unbroken vistas were designed to end with handsome, imposing public buildings like the Capitol and the College of William and Mary.

Roses tumble over the picket fence of this formal topiary garden.

Colonists were fascinated with botany and sent specimens of new plants found in America back to England to be studied. Plants, seeds, and cuttings were also brought over on many ships to be tested in the Virginia soil.

The colonists' love of order was reflected in carefully kept yards as well as in the tidy symmetry of Williamsburg's buildings.

GATES & FENCES

Tidy picket fences outline the gardens and greens of Williamsburg like thousands of white stitches in a verdant patchwork quilt. There are narrow pickets and wide ones, pickets shaped like arrows and others like M's. Some pickets are lost in masses of wisteria blossoms, others are entwined with Chero-

kee roses. Some provide a simple backdrop for perennial beds, others enclose the brick walks of formal gardens.

White picket gates are low and push open easily. Many swing shut by themselves, thanks to an ingenious closing device. A heavy metal ball is attached to a chain that goes from the gate to a post. When you let go of the gate, the weight of the ball will pull the gate shut.

Not all gates and fences are

made of white pickets. More stylish fences, like the one in back of the Wythe House, look like lacy ribbons. The fence around the Lightfoot House is of Chinese Chippendale design, considered the height of fashion for a time during the eighteenth century.

Crude, unpainted post-and-rail fences outline the fields behind the windmill and worm fences zigzag around pastures at the edge of the town. There are simple board fences with striking, horizontal

lines and others that form X's.

Trees and shrubs have been trained and pruned into fences. Look in the vegetable garden behind the King's Arms Tavern and find miniature fruit trees espaliered to enclose the rows of vegetables. Arches over gates are clipped out of thick hedges or formed with pleached, or interwoven, branches.

Stout brick walls surround the Governor's Palace, the Capitol, and Bruton Parish Church. The imposing gates in these walls are topped with spiked bars, setting those public buildings apart from less important structures, which have only pickets to guard them.

Fences were not just for decoration or protection. According to a town ordinance, house lots had to be enclosed by a fence in order to keep stray horses and cattle from wandering into private yards. Instead, they roamed freely in the streets!

The distinct lines of fences formed boundaries between individual lots but linked them together, too. Citizens of Williamsburg knew their enclosed land was their private property, but also part of a harmonious community. Williamsburg's fences—more than seven miles in all—are one more example of how the early colonists blended the practical with the pleasing, finding in the simple, functional objects of daily life an opportunity to enhance their environment.

One of the most beautiful and dignified homes in Williamsburg belonged to one of its most admired and accomplished citizens, George Wythe. A lawyer by profession, Wythe was also a judge, a member of the House of Burgesses, the teacher of Thomas Jefferson, a mayor of Williamsburg, and the first Virginian to sign the Declaration of Independence.

The stately brick house in which Wythe and his second wife, Elizabeth, lived is thought to have been designed by her father and stands as an example of colonial architecture at its finest. Step through the front door for a glimpse of their elegant home and imagine the refined lifestyle enjoyed by one of Williamsburg's most privileged families. When you are ready to leave these gracious rooms, go out through the back door, past the flower garden and into the yard beyond. Here, in contrast, you will find a miniature plantation, buzzing with activity: a kitchen and laundry, a stable and smokehouse, a lumber house and fowl house. Here, amid gardens, arbors, and orchards, the Wythe household rolled up its sleeves and got to work.

LUMBER
HOUSE

LAUNDRY

SMOKE
HOUSE

KITCHEN

WELL

GEORGE
WYTHE
HOUSE

KITCHEN GARDEN

I N THE KITCHEN the cook presided over the busy hearth, basting a juicy piece of meat on a spit, stirring a pot of fish chowder, pulling a pan of cinnamon buns from the oven. Preparing food for the Wythe household—or any large colonial household—was a never-ending job. The crowded, smoke-filled kitchen was a separate structure so that the main house would be free from the heat and odors of cooking.

Even on the most sweltering summer day, the fire was kept going to produce the bed of coals that provided the heat for cooking. Instead of placing a pot of food directly over the flames, it was usually put on a trivet on the hearth. The cooking temperature was controlled by raking coals under the trivet or pushing them back into the fire. Several trivets could be set up on the hearth at the same time so the colonial

The cook held the most responsible position in the operations of the colonial household. Her duties included planning meals with the mistress of the household, shopping for the food, and, of course, preparing it.

cook had a stove with an unlimited number of burners! Coals were also shoveled into ovens built into the walls of the chimney. A colonial cook tested the temperature of the oven with her arm. When the oven was hot enough, the coals were removed and the pie, cake, or bread was put in to bake. Meat was grilled on a spit—a long iron arm that could be raised or lowered over the coals. Large heavy pots hung from wrought-iron cranes that swung over the fire.

The cook had a plentiful variety of food to work with. Vegetable gardens and fruit orchards flourished in the rich Virginia soil. The nearby woods were full of game; the rivers teemed with fish; the beehives burst with honey. Cows, pigs, and chickens were raised in Williamsburg and on plantations outside of town.

Nearby Chesapeake Bay provided a bountiful supply of crabs, oysters, and clams. Delicacies like chocolate, coffee, and exotic fruits were imported and sold in Williamsburg's stores. Lump sugar, which came molded in the shape of a cone, was an imported item that was kept under lock and key!

Spoon Bread

Put one pint of milk on the fire and when it comes to a boil stir in two tablespoons of corn meal. Let cook until very thick stirring constantly. Cool, add three beaten eggs, two tablespoons of flour, one half teaspoon of salt, one tablespoon melted butter. Bake in buttered dish for thirty-five minutes in moderate oven.

Even the simplest ingredients took time to prepare. Butter had to be churned by hand and sugar scraped from a hard cone-shaped mold.

Feasting was an important part of any holiday celebration or special occasion. The cook prepared an elaborate array of specialties for meals that often lasted for hours.

The Wythe family probably started the day with breakfast between eight and nine o'clock. They might have tea, coffee, or hot chocolate, fruit, or porridge, and cold meat such as venison, game, or ham. Almost always there would be hot breads such as corn pone or Indian cakes. Dinner, served in the afternoon between two and three, was usually a big meal with at least two courses. The cook might prepare pea soup, a salad of fresh garden greens, roast potatoes, spice muffins, brandied peaches, calves' tongue, deviled crab cakes, and Virginia ham. Chicken and salted meats were everyday fare served in a variety of ways. Cider, wine, ale, or beer were the usual beverages. For dessert tempting puddings, cakes, and pies were offered or perhaps a pecan tart, rich and heavy as gold.

Around five o'clock Mrs. Wythe might entertain friends for tea in the parlor, serving small cakes or cookies. Tea was imported and expensive so teatime was probably not observed with the regularity it was in England. A light supper was served between eight and nine in the evening. It usually consisted of cold meat or leftovers from dinner. Leftovers were used quickly because there was no refrigeration and food might spoil if left overnight.

Holidays like Christmas and Easter and special events such as weddings and christenings were celebrated with elaborate feasts. To attend these events, friends and relatives often travelled for days—and occasionally stayed for weeks!

Ginger Cakes

Cream one-half cup of lard with two cups of brown sugar; stir in two cups of light molasses. Sift into this four cups of flour, two tablespoons of ginger, one-half teaspoon of salt, one teaspoon of soda. Add enough flour to make a stiff dough that can be rolled very thin. Cut with small round or fancy cutters and bake in buttered tins in a quick oven. They will burn easily.

IN THE GARDEN fat melons, pumpkins, squash, and vegetables grew in tidy profusion. Fragrant and spicy herbs for seasoning and preserving foods were gathered from the herb garden, then hung to dry in the lumber house, a storage building.

George Wythe, like many other eighteenth-century gentlemen, took great pride in his gardens. He had particular success with his grape arbor and apple trees. Other Williamsburg households grew cherries, peaches, and strawberries. Fresh fruit was a great treat. The cook preserved it in a variety of ways to keep a bit of that sunny summer taste for the winter. For example, cherries were dried, candied, pickled, stewed, or made into wine.

It was also necessary to preserve meat because it spoiled easily in the warm Virginia climate. Pork, beef, and fish were salted, doused with pepper or molasses, then hung in the smokehouse over a hardwood fire for several days. When you step inside this little building in back of the Wythe House, notice that it has thick walls, a dirt floor where the fire smoldered, and no chimney so smoke could not escape. The door is fastened with lock and key to keep the meat from being stolen.

Many Williamsburg households also had a dairy. It was a separate outbuilding designed with special vents and an underground storage area to keep milk, cream, and butter cool.

Many people were needed to keep the Wythe household operating smoothly. Slaves did the most. They worked in the gardens and in the many outbuildings, or dependencies, such as the kitchen, smokehouse, laundry, and stable.

 Because they kept no animals other than horses and poultry, the Wythes probably bought their meat from one of the two butchers in the city. However, within the city limits, other people raised cattle, pigs, goats, ducks, and geese. Almost every part of a butchered animal was used. Even a pig's bristles were used to make brushes.

The Wythes did keep chickens, pigeons, and doves—all considered excellent for eating. The doves lived in the dovecote next to the stable. It was high off the ground so that a servant could get at the nesting boxes easily from underneath. The chickens pecked all around the yard until the unlucky day they were chosen for the "fattening pen." There they ate well, moved little, and grew fat and tender. Eggs were collected from the hen coop when the chickens

Peach Marmalade

Take the ripest soft peaches (the yellow ones make the prettiest marmalade), pare them, and take out the stones; put them in the pan with one pound of dry, light-colored brown sugar to two of peaches; when they are juicy, they do not require water; with a silver or wooden spoon, chop them with the sugar; continue to do this, and let them boil gently till they are a transparent pulp, that will be a jelly when cold. Puffs made of this marmalade are very delicious.

were roosting. Chicken eggs were much smaller in the eighteenth century—only about half as big as they are now.

In the Wythe stable, next to the horses, you can see some of the family's vehicles. Being well-to-do, they had a carriage and a one-person "riding chair," which was a two-wheeled vehicle pulled by a horse. They also had a "well-built, handsome post-chariott" that they ordered from London in 1768. Saddles were expensive and made to order. The harnessmaker would measure the horse's back and the rider's backside, too, to be sure of a perfect fit.

George Wythe owned as many as eighteen slaves. The ones that worked on his property probably lived in the outbuildings, or they might have slept in the house on straw mattresses in the halls or in small spaces in the attic. Slaves ate in the kitchen, but their meals consisted of simpler food like hominy or ashcakes and leftovers from the Wythe's table. Wythe's slaves were probably given a day of rest each week. They generally had free time in the evening to enjoy family life.

The dovecote stands high above the garden fence behind the Wythe house.

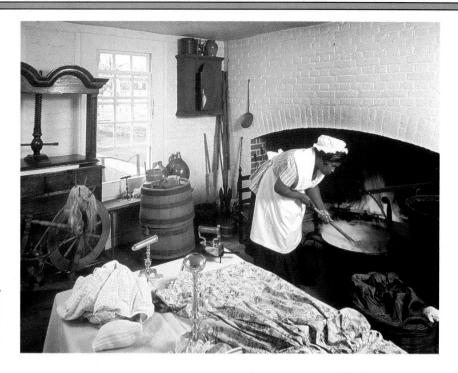

I N THE LAUNDRY across from the kitchen, steamy tubs full of sudsy water bubbled by the fire. The Wythes had a separate laundry house where the laundress would wash their linen, wool, or cotton clothing. Other people often sent their wash to a laundress in town because washing clothes and household linens was such a big job. The laundress had to haul water from the well, boil it over the fire, scrub the clothes with homemade soap, rinse them, wring them by hand, hang them on racks to dry, then starch, iron, mend, and fold them.

Household linens were heavy and awkward when wet, and stiff and full of stubborn creases when dry. Wrinkles were smoothed out of sheets and curtains in a linen press. Clothing was ironed with a handbox iron. Handbox irons had a removable piece of metal that was heated in the coals of the fire and then slipped inside the iron itself. A special iron called a *goffer* was used for ironing ruffles.

The Wythes were well-to-do people, so most of their clothes were probably made of materials like silk, velvet, and brocade. Those fabrics were not washed but instead were spot cleaned. For example, to remove a spot of grease, the laundress might rub it with a bit of bread or a special cleaning compound called Fuller's Earth. Garments were aired or kept in a

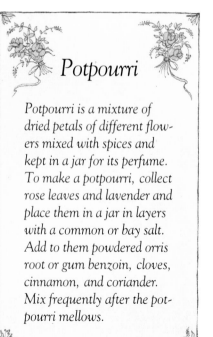

Potpourri

Potpourri is a mixture of dried petals of different flowers mixed with spices and kept in a jar for its perfume. To make a potpourri, collect rose leaves and lavender and place them in a jar in layers with a common or bay salt. Add to them powdered orris root or gum benzoin, cloves, cinnamon, and coriander. Mix frequently after the potpourri mellows.

The proper care of clothing was a year-round routine and probably the major responsibility of one or two household servants.

drawer with a sachet of flower petals called potpourri or a pomander ball of spices to keep them smelling fresh and to prevent moths.

The servants' clothing and many of the household linens were probably made of coarse imported fabrics or simple homespun material. Simple, that is, when compared to more elegant fabrics, but certainly not simple when one remembers the skill and work necessary to make homespun. First, wool was shorn from the sheep, and flax and cotton were gathered from gardens and fields. Then, the fibers had to be soaked, washed, dried, and carded, or combed, to untangle them. Next, the fibers were twisted together on a spinning wheel to make yarn or thread. Most women, rich and poor alike, knew how to spin. In

Spinning was a commonplace activity for all women. However, dying and weaving were usually the work of specialized people and did not often take place within the colonial household.

the wealthy households of Williamsburg, however, most of the yarn was spun by slaves. There were also "spinsters" for whom spinning was a profession.

Once enough wool yarn or cotton thread was spun, it was dipped in vats of dye that had been boiled over a fire. Brown dye was made from walnut hulls, blue from the indigo plant, and yellow from apple bark. Finished yarn was knit into caps or mittens. Finished thread was woven on looms into sturdy homespun fabric used for sacks, blankets, and clothing.

Not many houses had their own looms. Working-class people shared a loom with their neighbors or took their wool or thread to a professional weaver. In fact, homespun, the predominant fabric of the time, was not always

spun or woven at home. It was available in stores in Williamsburg, and many people purchased it instead of spending all the time and effort to make their own.

Clothing was acquired in many different ways. Ready-made garments could be ordered from England or purchased from the milliner or in stores. Fabric was often taken to a tailor to be made into clothing for a man. A woman's

clothing was made by a dressmaker, called a *mantuamaker*. A slave who had mastered fine stitching might sew clothes for the women and children in the family and would probably make the clothing for other slaves. Most women could sew well and added finishing touches to their own clothes. Colonial people had few clothes by today's standards, and the items they did have often had to last for years.

A LEISURE the Wythe family and their guests had many amusements. Friends would gather in their parlor to play music, sing, or even dance. Most ladies and gentlemen in the eighteenth century knew how to play an instrument—not for performing in front of an audience but for their own pleasure. Music teachers in Williamsburg provided instruction in the flute, violin, harpsichord, and guitar.

Other diversions included charades, cards, chess, board games, and puzzles. People read aloud to each other—poetry, the classics, or the Bible. Conversation would surely be a pleasure in the home of a man as learned and involved as George Wythe, with topics including history, science, gardening, philosophy, the law, and, of course, politics. Outdoor activities such as garden walks, lawn bowling, and badminton were popular. Carriage rides in the

Pecan Confections

Beat one egg white to a stiff froth; add gradually one cupful of brown sugar, one pinch of salt, one level tablespoonful of flour. Stir in one cupful of chopped pecans; drop on greased tins by small spoonfuls far apart. Bake in very slow oven for fifteen minutes. Remove from tin when partly cooled. Makes two dozen.

country were also a pleasurable pastime.

Eighteenth-century children played with marbles and wooden toy animals, rolled hoops, ran sack races, flew kites, fished, and played cricket. Little girls practiced their cross-stitches on samplers as soon as they were old enough to manage a needle.

Ladies' hands were never idle. They always had embroidery, needlepoint, crewelwork, sewing, or knitting to keep them busy.

Just follow the signs to the dozens of shops that are tucked between the houses and taverns on Duke of Gloucester Street. Citizens of colonial Williamsburg could find almost anything they wanted here—from a hoe to a hair ribbon! Many items sold in the shops were imported, but there was also a demand for locally made products. Colonists relied on a variety of talented individuals to make or repair the goods they needed. Today you can see more than a dozen skilled artisans creating products of lasting beauty, putting the same patience and pride into their work as their predecessors did more than two hundred years ago.

Apothecary

Stop in the apothecary's shop to see the drugstore of eighteenth-century Williamsburg. The apothecary was a pharmacist, a doctor, and sometimes a surgeon as you can tell from one look at his well-stocked shop. The shelves are crowded with urns and bottles containing the pharmacist's peculiar ointments, herbs, extracts, and elixirs. For his medical practice, the apothecary relied on an impressive collection of scientific books, and if surgery was necessary, he had all the very latest—and rather intimidating—surgical instruments. Imagine those operations with no anesthesia!

Some of the apothecary's cures seem logical to us. He might have prescribed licorice lozenges for a sore throat or tea made from home-grown herbs for a stomachache. Other cures and practices seem odd. The apothecary may have recommended sewing herbs into a cap to ease a headache. He might have coated pills with ground gold or a bright red powder made from crushed beetles! Ask to see the leeches he used for "bleeding" people.

MILLINER

A few steps away you will find a small department store run by the milliner. In the eighteenth century ladies and gentlemen came here to buy everything they needed to be fashionable.

In the glass-covered cases you can see fine linen handkerchiefs, dainty gloves, necklaces, fans, combs, and lovely imported fabrics for the ladies. The shelves are stocked with silver shoe buckles, fancy embroidered waistcoats, ruffled shirts, and purses—for the gentlemen! The well-dressed colonial gentleman in Williamsburg was quite a peacock.

Everyone wore hats in the eighteenth century. In the millinery you can see a butterfly cap, a collapsible calash, and even a "pudding cap" for wobbly toddlers. Triangular boxes are stacked on shelves to hold the most popular hat of all, the tricorn or "cocked" hat.

Fashionable colonists wanted to keep up with changing styles from Europe. Because clothing was imported and expensive, they would keep a dress or coat for a long time, but update it at the millinery. Here they could purchase a new feather for a hat, new trim for the sleeves of a coat, or even a whole new front for a dress called a *stomacher*.

And how did the colonists know what the newest fashions were in Europe? Those serious-looking, well-dressed dolls on the milliner's shelves showed the colonists what stylish Londoners and Parisians were wearing. The dolls' clothes, perfect in every detail, showed how low necklines were cut, how full skirts were, and how hats should be trimmed.

SMITHS

Pungent smoke and the ringing of hammers often fill the air in Williamsburg. Follow them and you will probably find the town's blacksmith hard at work. The blacksmith's enormous, creaking bellows enabled him to control the fire so that he could soften the heavy pieces of black iron and shape them into utensils and tools like hoes, bootscrapers, and cooking spits. Many of the craftspeople in Williamsburg depended on the blacksmith. He made hinges for the carpenter, barrel hoops for the cooper, metal tires for the wheelwright, pressing irons for the laundress, castors for the cabinetmaker, and long-handled spoons for the baker.

Almost everyone needed the blacksmith, but the silversmith had only a small, wealthy clientele. Silver was precious so the silversmith became adept at repairing and reshaping the treasured silver bowls, teapots, cups, and spoons. He also sold jewelry, shoe buckles, and buttons, which he imported or made in his own shop. The tap-tap-tap of the silversmith's hammer echoes the tick-tick-tick of the clocks and watches in his cases. Because the silversmith of Williamsburg had a delicate touch and precision tools, he was the one who repaired clocks and watches.

The gunsmith had to master several crafts to make guns "lock, stock, and barrel." He had to know the blacksmith's trade to forge a gun barrel out of a bar of iron. He had to be a competent woodcarver to form the handle or stock. And he needed the precise skills of the silversmith to fit and engrave the trigger and flintlock. Because all free white men over sixteen were required by law to own a gun in colonial Williamsburg, this smith stayed busy making and maintaining firearms for the entire community.

BARBER

Step across the street to the barber's shop at the sign of the red-and-white-striped pole. Here is where the eighteenth-century gentleman went to have his whiskers shaved, his hair trimmed, and his wig, or peruke, made. Wigs were very fashionable in colonial Williamsburg. The few ladies who wore wigs had them cared for at home, but gentlemen put their heads in the hands of the barber.

A busy gentleman might have a wooden model made of his head, which he'd leave at the barber's shop so the barber could fit the wig perfectly. Wigs were made of horsehair, goat hair, or human hair sewn into a tight-fitting cap. Often a gentleman would have his whole head shaved so that this cap would fit snugly. If his wig got disheveled, the gentleman would bring it to the barber's shop to be clipped, cleaned, combed, and braided. If the curls were drooping, the hair was wrapped on wooden rollers, boiled in water, and baked in an oven. Of course, only a wealthy, important man could afford a thick wig with lots of curls. One look told everyone he was a "big wig."

For fancy occasions a gentleman dusted his wig with white powder. Often the wig needed to be re-dusted during the evening. The Governor's Palace had a powder room just for this purpose!

PRINTER & BOOKBINDER

Walk down the steep steps into the small courtyard between the printing office and the book bindery. It seems peaceful but don't let the quiet fool you. You are standing in the middle of the most important communications center in colonial Virginia. If controversial ideas had voices, this courtyard would still be ringing with echoes from the eighteenth century.

Because the printed word was the best way to communicate over long distances, Williamsburg's printing complex—the post office, printing office, and book bindery—was the clearinghouse for information. People came to the post office to pick up letters, packages, and messages as there was no home mail delivery in the eighteenth century. Important notices and advertisements were posted on the walls there, too.

Downstairs the giant printing press turned out Virginia's first newspaper, the *Virginia Gazette*, as well as books, proclamations, posters, and controversial political pamphlets. Williamsburg's printer was appointed public printer by the government of Virginia and was responsible for printing documents for the General Assembly. In the book bindery books of law, medicine, poetry, and philosophy were assembled by hand.

THE COMMUNITY OF WILLIAMSBURG

The city of Williamsburg came to life in its public buildings. In shops people met to gossip and visit. In taverns they gathered to discuss news and make merry. At the church they worshiped together and at the college they studied. They made laws in the Capitol and enforced them at the Courthouse. At the Powder Magazine the militia marched. At Palace balls the gentry danced.

Wherever people gathered—to attend to ordinary daily tasks or participate in organized institutions of religion, education, and government—they exchanged ideas and common concerns. Whenever people gathered, they were creating something new: the community of Williamsburg.

STORES

You could bring a long shopping list to any of the stores in colonial Williamsburg. They were the one-stop shopping centers of the eighteenth century. Tarpley's, Prentis's, and Greenhow's stores offered their customers a great variety of merchandise. Some of it was locally made by Williamsburg's craftspeople, but most was imported through or from England. There were teapots from China, leather from London, tulip bulbs from Holland, and spices from the West Indies. There were cloaks, aprons, sugar, buckets, pottery, seeds, brooms, nails, iron kettles, chisels, buttons, and children's whistles.

Residents of Williamsburg might have shopped twice a week, though people from farther away may have come to town only twice a year. A shopkeeper like John Greenhow usually served fewer than ten customers a day. He would give all of his customers patient, personal attention. He might hold a bolt of blue cotton up to the window so that they could check its color in the sunlight or let them feel the slippery smoothness of some fine satin ribbon. He would help them find the right-sized garden rake and the sharpest file, let them sniff scented soaps, taste candied almonds, and carefully measure scoops of rice or flour for them.

Colonists could pay for their purchases with a coin made in England for use in Virginia. However, most shoppers used Dutch or Spanish coins that were weighed to determine how much they were worth. John Greenhow advertised that he dealt with "ready money only," which meant cash. Some shopkeepers were willing to barter goods for grain. Others were willing to take back "tobacco notes," extending credit against the expected sale of the customer's tobacco crop.

It was probably in the shops and stores of colonial Williamsburg that frequent mumblings of dissatisfaction with British rule were uttered. Here the colonists were confronted with the high prices that resulted from the self-serving trade policies of England. In order to insure that locally made products did not erode the market for English goods, the British Parliament prohibited the colonists from manufacturing finished goods made in the colonies that might compete with products made in or imported through England. In addition, the British government also levied heavy taxes. For years people in all of the colonies abided by the laws laid down by the king and Parliament and paid the high prices that resulted from these trade policies and taxes. In time, however, the resigned sighs of individual shoppers exploded into the angry threat, "No taxation without representation," and a group of hot-headed patriots threw a shipload of taxed tea into Boston Harbor. Word of the Boston Tea Party rippled through the colonies and made its way to Williamsburg. One can only imagine the reactions of the shoppers in Tarpley's, Greenhow's, and Prentis's stores.

TAVERNS

If you had visited Williamsburg during Publick Times in the eighteenth century, you might have had difficulty finding room in one of the taverns. Although there were more than ten taverns located near the Capitol, sleeping space was limited. Very likely you would have had to share your bed with a stranger—or two! And if you were a woman, you would have had to stay with a friend in a private home as ladies did not usually stay in taverns.

Even if your bedfellow didn't snore or steal the quilted covers, it would have been difficult to get to sleep. Your bed could have been in a room with two or three other beds, or in a hallway where servants hurried by with trunks, chamber pots, or logs for the fire. Laughter, music, and the smell of food would drift up from downstairs.

Williamsburg's taverns may not have been the best place to go for a good night's sleep, but they were fine places for merrymaking, serious business, or catching up on the news. In large, cheerful public dining rooms such as that at Christiana Campbell's tavern, hungry travelers enjoyed hearty, plain fare. The meals, served on pewter plates with plenty of ale to drink, were inexpensive and filling. After dinner tavern guests might play a lively game of billiards or gather in front of the fire in the barroom for cards, dice, or conversation. Taverns offered "gambols and diversions" with entertainment by customers who

were musicians or singers. In such places as the Daphne Room of the Raleigh Tavern, private parties met for more elegant dinners where imported delicacies and fine wine were served. Balls held in the Apollo Room of the Raleigh rivaled those at the Governor's Palace.

Taverns were noisy during the day, too. The front passage was always a busy place with people constantly arriving and departing. Sometimes public auctions of land, goods, and slaves took place in front of the Raleigh. People with business to discuss might arrange to meet at the Bull's Head Room in Wetherburn's Tavern and seal their bargain with a glass of Henry Wetherburn's rum punch.

Taverns were information centers where advertisements and notices were posted to catch your eye. The tavern keeper served as a postmaster, holding packages, letters, and messages in his office for trav-

elers and townspeople. Tavern visitors from out of town brought the latest news and gossip.

In many ways there was no better place to measure the sentiment of the Williamsburg community than at its taverns. There, in a relaxed and convivial atmosphere, honest feelings could be expressed to friends and neighbors. After meetings at the Capitol the burgesses often retired to the taverns to relax and talk about the debates that had occurred in the House of Burgesses. During one particularly memorable evening at the Raleigh Tavern, the burgesses formally reassembled and voted to boycott English goods as a protest against the king's policies. Word of their daring decision must have leapt through Williamsburg and beyond, as tavern guests dispersed and carried the important news of the evening's events back to the community.

BRUTON PARISH CHURCH

Bruton Parish Church was one place in Williamsburg where members of all classes gathered—artisans, slaves, students, and wealthy landowners. They did not mix, however. Prestigious people sat in the front of the main section of the church in high-backed pews. You can see the names of Washington, Marshall, Monroe, Henry, and Jefferson on the pews there. Students sat in the west gallery, where you can find some of their initials carved in the handrail. Slaves sat in the north gallery.

Church attendance was required by law. Colonists who missed church had plenty of time to think about it in the pillory or the stocks, where they were sent for punishment. People were expected to support the church through a tax on the workers in a household, called a *tithe*.

There was no separation of church and state in colonial Williamsburg. The Anglican Church was the established church in the colony of Virginia endowed by law with a privileged status denied other religious groups. Because of this unique status, the clergy of Bruton Parish Church were a powerful force in the community. Ministers sometimes expressed strong views from the pulpit, especially at Publick Times when burgesses and appointed Council members were in town and a captive audience in the congregation.

Within the community the church was a respected neutral ground for those who were loyal to the king and for those who dissented from his policies. When Parliament closed the Port of Boston as punishment for the Boston Tea Party, burgesses in Williamsburg showed their support for the Massachusetts colonists by setting aside a day of fasting and prayer in Bruton Parish Church. It was a quiet but effective way to send their message of dissent to the king.

COLLEGE OF WILLIAM & MARY

For most children in the eighteenth century, an education was as far out of reach as the weather vane high atop the cupola of the Wren Building at the College of William and Mary. There were few free schools in the colony of Virginia, and many people never learned to read or write. Some young people became apprentices to learn a trade. Apprenticeship agreements usually called for instruction in reading, writing, and sometimes ciphering, but formal education was primarily for the privileged. Boys from wealthy families were tutored, and some were sent to England to study. Their sisters were tutored at home.

The wealthy citizens of Virginia were more fortunate than people in most other colonies for the College of William and Mary was located in Williamsburg. It was founded in 1693 and named after the king and queen. It had a grammar school for boys aged twelve to sixteen, an Indian school, and schools of philosophy and divinity. The maximum yearly enrollment of the college was approximately one hundred students. Fewer than forty boys were enrolled in the grammar school at any one time. They rose at dawn, put on their long black gowns, and gathered for prayers and breakfast. Classes met from seven to eleven in the morning and again after dinner from two until five. Students were expected to study mathematics, geography, and penmanship, write papers and give speeches in Greek and Latin. At seventeen they might enroll in the school of philosophy, as Thomas Jefferson did, where for four years they would study courses such as logic, ethics, rhetoric, and natural science.

The eighteenth century was a time of exciting new ideas, and the College attracted some of the most intellectual and learned men in the colony to Williamsburg. It also provided an arena where the new political and philosophical ideas that were fermenting in the community could be discussed, not the least of which was the need for a government responsive to the people.

COURTHOUSE OF 1770

Beauty contests? Acrobats? Foot races? Exotic animals? If you were standing in Market Square on a Fair Day, you might have seen all those attractions in colonial Williamsburg. Market Square, the broad green on either side of Duke of Gloucester Street, was a lively outdoor center of community life where the militia assembled, cows grazed, and at least twice a week country farmers set up an open-air market to sell their products.

However, for those who came to be tried in the Courthouse, a trip to Market Square was no cause for celebration. Two courts for the community of Williamsburg met there monthly: the James City County Court and the hustings, or city court. The county court handled all sorts of civil cases and criminal misdemeanors. More serious crimes such as murder, robbery, and arson were handled in the General Court, which met in the Capitol. However, most of the cases argued in both the county court and the General Court were civil cases about violations of apprenticeship agreements, broken contracts, disputes over land boundaries, and, especially, suits for payment of debts.

The other court that met on Market Square, the hustings court, dealt with infractions against the laws of the city of Williamsburg. If you were found guilty of drunken and disorderly behavior, gossiping, or unladylike language, you'd be sentenced here and clapped in the stocks or pillory for public humiliation. The respect of the community was so highly valued in colonial Williamsburg that it was often considered punishment enough to be embarrassed in front of your friends and your neighbors.

GAOL

The gaol is a jail. The spelling is different, but the pronunciation and the meaning are the same. Williamsburg had a gaol because the colony courts met here and accused criminals were held in gaol before being tried.

Prisoners accused of a crime slept on straw in an unheated cell and were given salt beef and ground meal to eat. If they weren't riveted into leg irons or arm cuffs by the blacksmith, they might be allowed to walk in the yard and talk to other prisoners during daylight hours. If they had money, they could buy better food and even liquor. Debtors imprisoned here for failure to pay their bills fared slightly better. They were given a mattress to sleep on in a cell heated by a fireplace.

The gaoler and his family lived in modest but comfortable quarters in a separate section of the gaol. Gaolers were not paid enough to live on and usually had another job. Peter Pelham, for example, was a gaoler and an organist at Bruton Parish Church. He made his other job easier by bringing a prisoner to church with him to pump the organ!

Prisoners sometimes had to wait in the gaol for several months until the General Court convened, which happened twice a year at Publick Times. Once judged, however, few criminals languished in prison. Colonial justice was efficient, and it was customary to empty the gaol after each meeting of the General Court. Criminals were punished, not imprisoned for rehabilitation. Sometimes, for certain pathetic cases juries were lenient or the governor granted an occasional pardon. Usually though, if found guilty, criminals were fined, lashed, mutilated, or branded. Hanging was the penalty for arson, piracy, horse stealing, forgery, burglary, and murder. The most infamous inmates of Williamsburg's gaol were Blackbeard's pirates, thirteen of whom were hanged after their trial in the General Court.

GOVERNOR'S PALACE

The Governor's Palace at the end of the wide, tree-lined Palace Green is solid, imposing, and elegant—everything the official residence and headquarters of the king's representative in the colony should have been. It served as a constant reminder to the Williamsburg community of the power of the king in America.

Usually a favored English lord was rewarded by the king with the appointment of governor. However, from 1699 to 1775 only three of the nine appointed governors actually came to Virginia and lived in the Palace. The others stayed in England and used their position to increase their personal wealth by collecting the governor's salary as well as a portion of the revenues that the crown drew from the colony. A lieutenant governor was sent to perform the duties in Williamsburg. Most of the resident governors and lieutenant governors were well respected and well liked, and many of them made significant contributions to the community. For example, Francis Nicholson drew up the town plan that gave Williamsburg its distinctive look. Alexander Spotswood designed several public buildings including Bruton Parish Church and the Powder Magazine. He directed the construction of the Palace and helped pay for its fish pond and terraced gardens with his own funds.

A governor's duties were serious ones. He spoke for the king when he presided over meetings of the Council and General Court in the Capitol. On behalf of the king he could dissolve and dismiss the House of Burgesses, effectively limiting its power. The governor was not a leader to be taken lightly as the military might of England stood behind him. Colonists were reminded of this power when they stepped into the entrance hall of the Palace. It was decorated with swords, pistols, muskets, and

flags, arranged in stunning, decorative patterns but looking formidable, nonetheless.

The wealth of the governor or lieutenant governor was evident from the furnishings of the Palace, most of which were his own personal property. The pantry was filled with linens, silver, gold cutlery, imported china, and crystal. Throughout the Palace, rooms were richly decorated with crimson damask, gilt and gold, mahogany and velvet. Furniture, rugs, decorations, curtains, and art imported from around the world reflected the latest style in England. The lovely formal gardens behind the Palace were patterned after the grand gardens favored by King William in England. Inside and out the Governor's Palace was the epitome of fashion.

An invitation to the Palace was an honor, not only because of the political distinction of meeting the king's representative, but also because the governor was at the top of the social hierarchy. Only the most prominent and fashionable people attended balls there. After dinner the governor's guests might listen to a string quartet play the newest music from Europe, dance in the ballroom under the light of glittering glass chandeliers, or sip punch and stroll through the ballroom garden.

Governor Botetourt was one of the most popular of all royal governors. After his death in 1770 he was so mourned that shops sold wax medallions of him. Yet the next Palace resident, Lord Dunmore, fled one night in June of 1775, ending forever the line of royal governors in Virginia. Why did Dunmore make such a hasty and ignominious exit? The answer lies less with the governors as individuals than with the increasingly independent colonists. In the community of Williamsburg and throughout the colony of Virginia, there was mounting impatience with the British government that the royal governor represented.

POWDER MAGAZINE

It's quiet at the Powder Magazine now. Occasionally a musket is fired or the rhythmic beat of the fife and drum corps disturbs the air. But in 1775, just as the sounds of war were heard in Massachusetts, a noisy incident here rumbled like distant thunder, warning colonists and British alike that revolution was about to explode.

Because Great Britain did not keep a professional standing army in Virginia, the colonists were responsible for their own protection against pirate raids, local riots, Indian attacks, and slave revolts.

For this purpose the colonists established militias, bands of citizen soldiers that were not trained as regular army units. Every able-bodied free white man from sixteen to sixty was obliged by law to serve in it. In 1715 a Powder Magazine was built as a storehouse for the colony's gunpowder and military equipment. It was located on Market Square where the militia mustered, or assembled for drills.

During March of 1775 representatives of the colonists gathered in Richmond for the second Vir-

ginia Convention. Perhaps they knew then that differences with the king could not be resolved peaceably. Armed confrontation with the British seemed inevitable so they voted to train the local militia with more discipline and care. When word of this decision reached Governor Dunmore at the Palace, he ordered a small group of his marines to remove the gunpowder from the Powder Magazine on Market Square. Under cover of darkness the men obeyed his orders but were spotted by some colonists.

Drums woke the city as the shout went out that the British were stealing the colony's gunpowder. Patrick Henry led a group of angry volunteers to demand return of the gunpowder or payment for it.

Dunmore protested that he had only removed the gunpowder for the colonists' own protection, claiming that he had been warned of a slave revolt. Nevertheless, payment was made to the colonists.

The gunpowder confrontation was a small incident; no shots were fired, no lives lost. But its significance was enormous. It was an unmistakable sign that the colonists of Virginia had finally had enough. They had tried peaceful protests—speeches, boycotts, prayers, and fasting—but the king and Parliament simply did not listen or would not respond. The people of Williamsburg, as part of the larger colonial community in America, had begun to realize that there was no choice but to risk their property and their lives to fight for the principles they believed in and the freedom for which they yearned.

THE CAPITOL

Perhaps no place in Williamsburg is haunted by more fascinating ghosts than the Capitol. It is here that Patrick Henry delivered the impassioned speeches that ignited Washington, Jefferson, and other patriots to action against the rule of the king and Parliament who had grown arrogant in their use and abuse of power. It is here—in a building whose architecture symbolically represents unity and accord—that the first cries of discord were heard, cries that ultimately brought down the powerful rule of the king of England in America.

The Capitol where the colonial legislature met was built in the shape of an *H*. On one side is the Hall of the House of Burgesses, a large, plainly decorated room where dark wood panelling contrasts starkly with white plaster. Burgesses were elected representatives from throughout the colony, chosen by white male landowners since only they could vote. Upstairs, on the other side of the *H*, the Governor's Council met in a room that had woodwork fashionably decorated in gilt and imitation marble. The Council was made up of twelve prominent Virginians appointed by the king to advise the governor. They sat in ornately carved high-backed chairs around a long oval table that was covered in a thick, richly patterned cloth. The crossbar of the *H*, the bridge between the two sides of the building, was appropriately a conference room. Here, burgesses and Council members gathered together as the General Assembly to pray and to resolve their differences. Downstairs in the General Courtroom people who broke the laws of the colony were tried by Council members who also served as judges in the highest court in the colony.

In the early days of colonization the Council members and the burgesses governed the colony together with the governor. But as time passed the governor and Council lost power to the burgesses, who voiced the objections of the people they represented. With increasing assertiveness the burgesses argued against the restrictive practices of the British government and its unilateral power to make laws and levy taxes.

In 1765 Parliament passed the Stamp Act, a law taxing publications and legal documents in the colonies. The colonists were enraged. They were not represented in Parliament and therefore had no say in the formulation of these policies. Patrick Henry spoke with passion against this taxation with-

out representation before the House of Burgesses. Other patriots joined him and eventually their outraged cries resulted in a boycott of British goods. Parliament repealed the Stamp Act in 1766.

At other times, when rhetoric and boycotts failed to move the king and Parliament, the colonists simply defied them. In 1769 another tax, the British Revenue Act, had been imposed on the colonists. When the House of Burgesses opposed it, the royal governor, as was his right, dissolved the House of Burgesses. This bold act only infuriated the burgesses more. With equal boldness they reconvened in the Raleigh Tavern and again voted to boycott British goods.

By May of 1776 the burgesses felt that nothing less than full freedom from the king's rule would do. In a special meeting they voted unanimously to adopt the Virginia Resolutions for Independence. It laid the groundwork for the Declaration of Independence, which was signed in Philadelphia and proclaimed just two months later from the steps of the Courthouse on Market Square. From that moment on Williamsburg was changed forever. No longer capital of the king's largest colony, it was the capital of a new commonwealth, free at last to govern itself.